A Visit to
AUSTRALIA

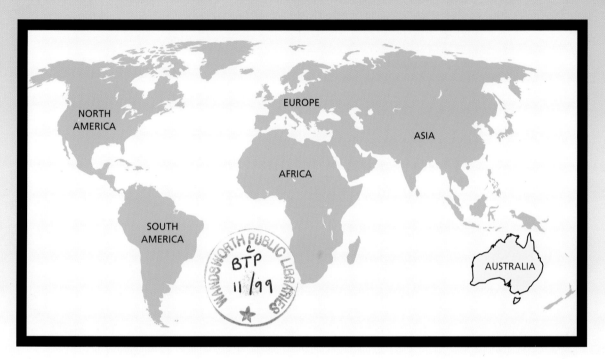

NORTH
AMERICA

EUROPE

ASIA

AFRICA

SOUTH
AMERICA

AUSTRALIA

Rachael Bell

Heinemann
LIBRARY

First published in Great Britain by Heinemann Library,
Halley Court, Jordan Hill, Oxford OX2 8EJ
a division of Reed Educational and Professional Publishing Ltd.

Heinemann is a registered trademark of Reed Educational & Professional Publishing Ltd.

OXFORD   MELBOURNE   AUCKLAND
JOHANNESBURG   BLANTYRE   GABORONE
IBADAN   PORTSMOUTH (NH) USA   CHICAGO

Designed by AMR
Illustrations by Art Construction
Printed in Hong Kong/China

03 02 01 00 99
10 9 8 7 6 5 4 3 2 1

ISBN 0 431 08343 6

British Library Cataloguing in Publication Data

Bell, Rachael
  A visit to Australia
  1.Australia – Juvenile literature
  I.Title II.Australia
  994

Acknowledgements
The Publishers would like to thank the following for permission to reproduce photographs:
Anthony Blake Photo Library, p. 13; Image Bank, (Simon Wilkinson) p. 14; J Allan Cash, pp. 7,
11, 17, 21, 24, 25; Opera Australia, p. 29; Robert Harding Picture Library, p. 16; (Rainbird) p. 20;
Spectrum Colour Library, p. 26; (B Lovell) p. 27; Trip, p. 10; (Eric Smith) pp. 5, 8, 9, 12, 19, 23;
(H Rogers) pp. 6, 22; (J Wakelin) p. 15; (J Cox) p. 18; (Australian Picture Library) p. 28.

Cover photograph reproduced with permission of Tony Stone (Paul Chesley)

Every effort has been made to contact copyright holders of any material reproduced in this
book. Any omissions will be rectified in subsequent printings if notice is given to the Publisher.

Any words appearing in bold, **like this**, are explained in the Glossary.

Contents

Australia

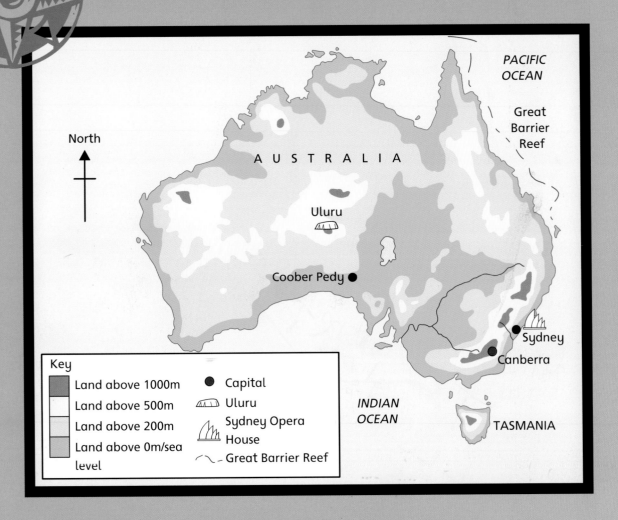

North

PACIFIC
OCEAN

A U S T R A L I A

Great
Barrier
Reef

Uluru

Coober Pedy ●

Sydney

Canberra

INDIAN
OCEAN

TASMANIA

Key

▨ Land above 1000m	● Capital
▢ Land above 500m	⌒ Uluru
▢ Land above 200m	Sydney Opera House
▢ Land above 0m/sea level	⌒ Great Barrier Reef

Australia is an island south of Asia.
Many other smaller islands are part of it.
It is a huge country but only 18 million
people live there.

The **Aborigines** have lived in Australia
for thousands of years. 200 years ago,
the British sent prisoners to live there.
In the last 100 years, people have moved
to Australia from Europe and Asia.

Land

Most of the land is flat and very dry.
There are few rivers. There are rainforests
in the north and mountains in the east.

Some parts of Australia are very hot.
Some parts get lots of rain. Most people
live in the south-east, where the summer
is hot and the winter is mild.

Landmarks

The most famous landmark is Uluru.
This is a huge rock that rises 348m
above the flat desert floor. It is very
special to the **Aborigines**.

The Sydney **Opera** House is also very
famous. It looks as if it is floating like
a ship on the water in Sydney Harbour.

Homes

Most people live in towns or cities.
The biggest city is Sydney. Many people
live outside the city in **modern** houses.

Homes in Coober Pedy are underground. This means they stay cool. The **Aborigines** gave the place this name. It means 'white man in a hole'.

Food

Barbecues are very popular because the weather is good. It is a quick and easy way to cook meat or fish and it is good fun to eat outside.

A new kind of Australian food is fusion food. This is a mixture of the different ways of cooking from all the different peoples in Australia.

Clothes

The weather is hot so people can wear
light beach clothes. Many people cover
themselves up because they do not want
to get sunburnt.

School uniforms are made from cotton
to keep the children cool. **Sun block** is
also part of the uniform. These children
at day care are wearing a special cap
that has a neck flap to keep the sun off.

Work

Australia makes about one-third of the world's wool. The sheep have lots of room to graze. Some **shearers** can shear as many as 95 sheep a day.

Australia has many **minerals** like diamonds, gold, iron and coal. Many people work in **mining** or **refining** them.

Transport

Australia has a railway right across it. But most goods and people travel by road. **Road trains** are the best way of getting sheep or cattle to the cities.

The most unusual transport system is the
Flying Doctor Service. These are ambulance
aeroplanes that fly to places in the **outback**.
People call them on a special radio.

language

The official language of Australia is English. But there are also older **Aboriginal** languages.

Many other languages are spoken in Australia, including Greek, Italian, Vietnamese, Thai, Chinese and Japanese.

School

Children have to go to school between the ages of 6 and 15. But most of them go between 5 and 17. One of the languages learned in schools is Japanese.

Children living in the **outback** have 'School of the Air'. They use the Flying Doctor Service radio to listen and speak to their teacher. They post their homework and go to a special summer school.

23

Free time

Outdoor sports like rugby, cricket and tennis are very popular in Australia. A special activity is **snorkelling** among the coral of the **Great Barrier Reef**.

Bush walking is becoming more and more popular. People find out more about the beautiful and unusual plants and animals of the bush.

Celebrations

The Melbourne Cup is a popular horse race. It is held on the first Tuesday in November. Some people dress up in silly costumes to go to the races.

January 26 is Australia Day. On that day in 1788, Captain Phillip sailed his ship into Port Jackson. He started the **settlement** that became Sydney.

The Arts

The **Aborigines** have old dances and
songs about how the world was made.
Aboriginal paintings are often made
in places that are **sacred** to them.

Concerts and plays are held at the Sydney **Opera** House. In most cities there are art galleries and museums.

Factfile

Name The full name of Australia is the Commonwealth of Australia.

Capital The **capital** of Australia is Canberra.

Languages The official language of Australia is English. There are many people who speak other languages: 2 out of 100 people speak Italian and 1 out of 100 people speak an **Aborigine** language.

Population There are about 18 million people living in Australia.

Money Australians have the Australian dollar.

Religions Most people are Christians, but there are some Muslims, Buddhists and Jews. The Aborigines have their own beliefs.

Products Australia **exports** more beef and lamb than any other country. It also makes lots of wheat, chemicals, iron, coal, wool, food and wine.

Words you can learn

These words are from the Wongatha language that is spoken by the Aborigines of the Western Desert. You say them just as they look.

goothoo	one	ngarla yoowa	please
gootharda	two	barloonthanoo	thank you
marngoodba	three	yoowa	yes
yoowa	hello	narthe	no
maa-bitha	goodbye		

Glossary

Aborigines	people who first lived in Australia
bush walking	camping and walking in any natural area
capital	the city where the government is based
explorer	somebody who travels to find new places
export	selling things to other countries
Great Barrier Reef	the collection of islands and coral reefs which are made up of millions and millions of the old shells or outer skeletons of the tiny coral animal. It looks and feels like rock.
minerals	rocks that are dug out of the earth because they are valuable or useful
mining	digging for minerals either on the earth's surface or deep underground
modern	new or up-to-date
opera	a play with music and singing
outback	the large areas of land that are almost deserts and where very few people live, except those living on sheep or cattle stations
refining	separating the minerals from the rocks which they come from
road trains	very long lorries, sometimes with 80 wheels
sacred	something that is special to a religion
settlement	a completely new town which is quickly built for people who have arrived from far away
shearers	the people who cut the wool off sheep
snorkelling	swimming underwater using a tube to breathe through
sun block	cream that stops you getting sunburnt

Index